Protecting Our Country

SERVING IN THE
COAST GUARD

Alix Wood

PowerKiDS
press

New York

Published in 2014 by Rosen Publishing
29 East 21st Street, New York, NY 10010

Editor for Alix Wood Books: Eloise Macgregor
Designer: Alix Wood
Researcher: Kevin Wood
Military Consultant: Group Captain MF Baker MA RAF (Retd)
Educational Consultant: Amanda Baker BEd (Hons) PGCDL

Photo Credits: Cover, 7 bottom, 8 © Shutterstock; 1, 4 bottom, 5, 6, 7 top and
middle, 9, 10, 11, 12, 13, 14, 15, 16, 17, 18, 19, 20, 21, 22, 23, 24, 25, 26,
27, 28, 29, 31 © Defenseimagery.mil; 4 top © US Government

Library of Congress Cataloging-in-Publication Data

Wood, Alix.
  Serving in the Coast Guard / by Alix Wood.
      pages cm. — (Protecting our country)
  Includes index.
  ISBN 978-1-4777-1298-6 (library binding) — ISBN 978-1-4777-1402-7 (pbk.) —
  ISBN 978-1-4777-1403-4 (6-pack)
  1. United States. Coast Guard–Juvenile literature. I. Title.
  VG53.W64 2014
  363.28'60973—dc23
                              2013002103

Manufactured in the United States of America

CPSIA Compliance Information: Batch #S13PK3: For Further Information contact Rosen Publishing, New York, New York at 1-800-237-9932

Contents

What Does the Coast Guard Do?

The armed services are made up of highly skilled and trained men and women who defend our country. The US Coast Guard is unique because it is involved with **law enforcement** as well. It operates under the Department of Homeland Security, but can transfer to the Department of the Navy if there is a war.

A member of the US Coast Guard **Maritime** Safety and Security Team, left, and a navy technician, right, prepare to board a ship.

The US Coast Guard often works closely with the US Navy. It provides law enforcement teams for naval operations if they need to arrest people or seize goods. It can help the navy guard ports and assets, like ships. The Coast Guard also helps the navy in a defense role. They will work together in search and rescue operations, too.

The US Coast Guard is made up of what used to be five separate agencies. They were the Revenue Cutter Service, the Lighthouse Service, the Steamboat Inspection Service, the Bureau of **Navigation**, and the Life-Saving Service. The services' duties often overlapped, so they were finally united as the Coast Guard.

The cutter USCGC *Eagle* passes Portland Head Light. The *Eagle* is the Coast Guard's training ship.

Search and Rescue

The Coast Guard's search and rescue teams aim to find anyone lost at sea and prevent loss of life. The Coast Guard has centers in Alaska, Hawaii, Guam, and Puerto Rico, as well as on the Great Lakes and inland US waterways.

Each Coast Guard unit is ready to go within 30 minutes of getting a call for help. Specialist equipment helps find people and vessels in the water. Units use **infrared** heat-seeking systems that can spot a heat source, such as a person, in the water. They have direction-finding radio equipment and night-vision goggles. The Coast Guard uses different search methods depending on the size of area that needs to be covered. The more times pilots and divers cover the same area, the higher their chance of finding someone is.

A life ring can be used as a float by someone in the water.

If someone vanishes at sea, the Coast Guard appoints a mission coordinator to run the search and rescue. They organize planes, helicopters, and boats, and assess the missing person's chances of survival. They use special software to look at water and air temperature, the person's height, weight, clothing, and time of disappearance, and if the person had a flotation device.

Coast Guard helicopter pilots are trained to be able to hover close to cliffs or over high seas while lowering a rescue swimmer.

FACT FILE

If you call the Coast Guard because you have seen a red distress **flare**, they will try to work out how far out to sea the flare was. To help them, hold your arm straight out in front of you and make a closed fist. Hold the bottom of your fist on the horizon with the thumb on top. Picture the flare that you saw and compare the height of it at its peak to your fist. Was it half a fist? A whole fist? Two fists? Using this information, the Coast Guard can estimate how far away the flare was from you and send help to the right place.

Horizon

Aiding Navigation

Waterways can be very busy. Aids to navigation are like street signs and traffic lights for vessels on the water. Lighthouses, buoys, and beacons act as signals alerting people to dangers and helping with navigation. The Coast Guard's Aids to Navigation Teams service small buoys, jetty lights, and lighthouses.

A lighthouse is a tower with a bright light at the top. It warns people in boats about dangerous areas. Lighthouse keepers used to have to keep the light lit. Automatic lamp changers made this job unnecessary. For many years, lighthouses still had keepers. This was partly because lighthouse keepers could serve as a rescue service. Modern lighthouses now usually use solar-charged batteries and are looked after by the Coast Guard.

Before electricity, lighthouse keepers had to keep the lamp alight at night. During an 8-hour watch, they had to climb the tower up to three times a night. Some lighthouses had two hundred steps!

When you are coming into port in North and South America, the red buoy markers are on your right and the green are on your left. An easy way to remember this is the phrase "red right returning." In many other countries, the colors are the other way around. The markers show where it is safe to travel.

A damage controlman cuts out a section of chain to replace a buoy's mooring.

Coast Guard ships' hulls are painted different colors depending on the job they do. The black hulls are the buoy tenders. Crew wear different colored hard hats. Red helmets are damage controlmen, white are buoy deck supervisors, blue are trained crew, and green is for rookies. The job is dangerous and challenging. The enormous, heavy buoys can become destructive wrecking balls if they are not carefully hoisted and controlled.

A team member climbs a tower to check the equipment.

Coast Guard Cutters

Originally, the Coast Guard used the term "cutter" in its traditional sense, as a type of small sailing ship. Today a Coast Guard cutter is any vessel which can accommodate a permanent crew and is 65 feet (20 m) or more in length.

Cutters are used for law enforcement, search and rescue, buoy tending, ice-breaking, and military defense. Life on a cutter is not easy. There is not much space and the crew spends an average of 185 days away from home each year.

Bridge

Gun

Helicopter deck

The captain runs the ship. A captain's personality can have a big effect on the character of the ship and the way a crew conducts itself. The captain (left) works mainly on the bridge, overseeing the ship.

After the day's work is over, everyone usually gathers to practice damage control. The crew is taught fire fighting, how to mend a boat and keep it from sinking, and basic first aid. This training is squeezed in between their normal eight-hour workday and eight hours of watch. It is important to know how to keep everyone safe if there is an emergency. No one could come to the cutter's aid in time out at sea.

Cutters usually have a smaller boat on board. Some cutters have helicopter flight decks. The crewmen (left) are running to tie down a Dolphin helicopter on the flight deck. The helicopter could be blown off the deck if they don't act quickly.

Law Enforcement

The Coast Guard has three main law enforcement missions. These are ensuring that import taxes are not avoided, protecting shipping from pirates, and **intercepting** illegal cargo.

Law enforcement cutters have white hulls.

The crews must have knowledge of seamanship, **diplomacy**, the law, and combat readiness. The Coast Guard enforces our drug, immigration, and fisheries laws. The Coast Guard also plays a role in maritime defense, providing port security, harbor defense, and coastal warfare operations.

Members of a visit, board, search, and seizure team hold suspected pirates after responding to a distress signal.

Coast Guard cutters have special **radar** detection systems that can spot suspicious boat traffic. Crew can use helicopters or the "hook and climb" method to get aboard suspicious ships. Their boat will pull alongside and they hook a collapsible ladder and rapidly board the ship.

FACT FILE

Boarding a ship can be dangerous. If the ship's crew has something to hide, they might resist. The boarding team carries firearms just in case. The team back on the cutter needs to keep close contact. Cameras and spotlights help them keep a lookout on the men and women sent to board the suspect vessel. Deck hands wait on the deck to pull their shipmates to safety after the mission.

USCGC *Eagle*

The Coast Guard has a special ship for training cadets and for goodwill trips around the world. The USCGC *Eagle* is an old **square-rigged** sailing vessel. Built in Germany in 1936, the ship was taken after World War II as a prize of war.

USCGC *Eagle* is the sixth Coast Guard cutter to bear the name. Originally operated by Nazi Germany to train cadets for the German navy, the ship was sailed to the US in 1947. The hull is made of thick steel, with two full-length steel decks. Some of the decks are made of teak. When in homeport in New London, Connecticut, *Eagle* rests near the US Coast Guard Academy. Everyone who attends the Academy sails on America's only active duty square rigger at some point.

Cadets learn to climb the **rigging** and navigate using the stars and a sextant (above). You can use a sextant to measure the angle between a star and the horizon. That angle, and the time when it was measured, can be used to work out where you are on a ship's chart.

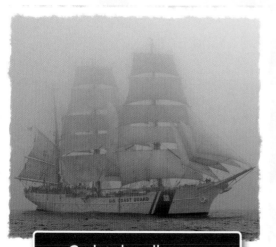

Cadets handle more than 20,000 square feet (1,858 sq m) of sail and 5 miles (8 km) of rigging.

Training on *Eagle* is a character-building experience. A permanent crew of six officers and 55 crew looks after the ship year-round and trains young coastguardsmen. The training is challenging. Working high in the rigging, cadets need to learn to overcome their fear. The experience helps them develop leadership and teamwork skills that are valuable throughout their careers.

Operations Specialists

Stationed throughout the country, Coast Guard operations specialists coordinate search and rescue operations, gather and analyze intelligence, and track and identify targets. Operations specialists are at the heart of almost every Coast Guard mission.

Operations specialists are always in the middle of the action, even though they can sometimes be miles away onshore in Rescue Coordination Centers. They may not be the ones who go out and pull someone out of the water, but they have a big part in accomplishing the mission. They do the navigation and planning. They also do the paperwork at the end.

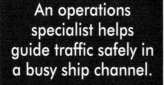

An operations specialist helps guide traffic safely in a busy ship channel.

Radio watchstanders monitor communication devices. This keeps a ship ready to handle any mission at any time. They send and receive all of the ships messages. They send and receive all of the ship's mail, too! They load codes which scramble messages so that only the Coast Guard can understand them. They fix any equipment problems. Radio watch is done 24 hours a day, 7 days a week while the ship is away from homeport.

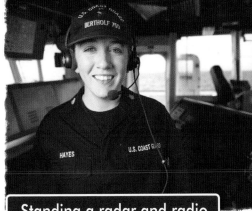

Standing a radar and radio watch on board ship.

Monitoring equipment for a search and rescue mission.

Protecting Our Environment

The Coast Guard's National Strike Force deals with environmental problems like oil and chemical spills and other hazardous materials in the water. There are Pacific, Atlantic, and Gulf Strike Teams.

Oils spills can be very harmful to wildlife. Since oil spreads over the surface of seawater, the Coast Guard lassoes giant puddles of oil with floating barriers called containment booms. Then, a skimmer **siphons** the oil from the water. The skimmer is controlled by someone on deck. The oil collected by the skimmer is pumped into an inflatable barge pulled behind the ship.

Containment boom

Skimmer

Oil and gas can be burnt off using a controlled burn (above). The spill is surrounded with a fire-resistant floating boom. The oil is then towed to a safe distance and set alight with a flare. A specialist monitors the burn closely.

The teams also deal with chemical, biological, and **radiation** leaks. They have equipment that can detect leaks and then clean up the area if one is detected. They have special protective clothing if needed.

Oil harms the feathers of birds and the fur of mammals. Birds' wings get too heavy and they can't fly. Animals that rely on scent to find each other can get lost as the smell of the oil covers up their natural scent. Seal pups can die of cold because their woolly fur no longer traps warm air to keep them warm. Rescuers use soap to remove oil, but it also removes the animals' natural waterproofing oils. The animals need to be kept safe until these oils are replaced.

A marine science technician with the Pacific Strike Team sets up the radiation detection equipment.

Coast Guard Aircraft

The Coast Guard uses aircraft to perform search and rescue, spot smugglers and illegal immigrants, and transport people and supplies. Most Coast Guard aircraft are helicopters.

For medium-range missions, the Coast Guard uses the Jayhawk helicopter. For shorter missions, it uses the Dolphin. While both helicopters are usually based on shore, they can also operate from the large cutters which have helipads. The Dolphin has an advanced automatic flight control system. It can be set to automatically hover at a certain distance above the ground or ocean surface. It can even be set to fly in preset search patterns.

Hoist

A Dolphin helicopter on a search and rescue mission.

The Jayhawk is designed to fly a crew of four and can fit up to six extra people on board. To the right, a Jayhawk helicopter hoists stranded crewmen from the mobile drilling unit Kulluk.

The Coast Guard also uses surveillance planes, transport planes, and jets. Below is a Hercules transport plane airdropping vital supplies to a Coast Guard cutter. The Coast Guard has been flying the Hercules since 1958!

FACT FILE

A precision airdrop is a way of getting supplies to ships when you can't land. Delicate supplies can be packaged in a waterproof and shatterproof rescue container. The aircrew flies over the ship and drops a trail line directly on the deck, followed by the rescue container which lands in the water. The container can then be pulled aboard by the trail line.

Accident Prevention

One of the Coast Guard's main roles is to promote boating safety. Boats have to be equipped with navigation lights, whistles, fire extinguishers, and life preservers by law.

The Coast Guard prefers to educate the public rather than punish them if they don't have the right equipment. The Coast Guard often visits schools and gives talks on boating safety. Students are taught the importance of wearing life jackets that fit properly. The students can try on life jackets. They will see that life jackets will slip off easily if they are too big and will not keep you afloat in the water if they are too small.

A girl tries on a life jacket during a school visit by the Coast Guard.

FACT FILE

This safety equipment is also useful: a first aid kit, a VHF radio, emergency flares, a tool kit, a bucket, oars or paddles, sunscreen, a copy of the navigational rule book, extra fuel and water, and an anchor with a long enough chain.

Coastie the Patrol Boat sometimes goes to schools to help teach the importance of wearing life preservers.

The Coast Guard offers free vessel safety checks for boat owners. They also board boats to check that the people aboard are following safety advice and the law.

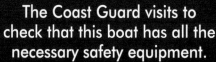

The Coast Guard visits to check that this boat has all the necessary safety equipment.

Boats

A Coast Guard boat is any Coast Guard vessel that is less than 65 feet (20 m) long. The Coast Guard operates about 1,400 boats.

The motor lifeboat, or MLB, is the Coast Guard's heavy-weather boat used for search and rescue as well as law enforcement and homeland security. The boats are virtually unsinkable and can turn themselves right side up if they capsize. They are designed to weather hurricane-force winds and heavy seas. They can be driven from either the open bridge or the enclosed bridge.

Open bridge

Enclosed bridge

Throttle

Driving on the open bridge

An MLB trains in the surf

The Long Range Interceptor (above) is fast. It is capable of catching suspicious vessels or reaching the scene of an emergency quickly. It can be carried on a cutter and launched so a boarding party or search and rescue team can leave the main ship for up to 10 hours. The cabin is climate controlled and has shock-absorbing seats. It can be armed with machine guns or grenade launchers.

FACT FILE

Boarding parties can be launched while the vessel is underway from the cutter's stern launching ramp. The cutter (right) is carrying a Rigid Hull Inflatable Boat, or RHIB. It can be launched and retrieved by a single crewmember on deck.

RHIB

U.S. COAST GUARD

Unmanned Craft

An unmanned aerial vehicle, or UAV, is an aircraft without a human pilot on board. It is also called a drone. An ROV is a remotely operated vehicle which can operate underwater. They are both either controlled by computers in the vehicle, or via remote control by an operator on the ground or in another vehicle.

UAVs and ROVs will play an larger role in Coast Guard search and rescue in the future. The Predator UAV can provide photograph like images through clouds, rain, or fog, day or night, all in real time. The Guardian UAV is equipped with a marine search radar.

A crewmember releases a Scan Eagle. This UAV is launched using a catapult. It is retrieved using the hooks on its wings and a line. This type of drone can be used for **reconnaissance**.

Tilt rotor

An electronics technician heaves an ROV into the water.

The ROV's controls

The ROV is an unmanned, highly maneuverable underwater video and data robot. It is used to help the Coast Guard inspect piers and vessels, do search and recovery, and detect improvised explosive devices. The ROV is linked to the ship by a tether which contains cables. These carry electrical power, video, and data signals back and forth between the operator and the vehicle.

Combating Weather

The Coast Guard often has to respond to extreme weather. It has icebreakers to help vessels and communities cut off by ice. It provides accurate weather reports for shipping and is often called on to provide services after weather disasters such as hurricanes.

The Coast Guard operates the only US heavy icebreakers capable of providing year-round access to the polar regions. It also operates the International Ice Patrol. In 2008, that organization supplied information on 1,029 icebergs that could be a danger to shipping. Scientists also use the ships as a base for conducting research.

An icebreaker breaks a channel to the McMurdo Station to allow supply ships to get through.

U. S. COAST GUARD

The Coast Guard broadcasts marine weather forecasts continuously. The broadcasts use a **synthesized** voice known as "Iron Mike." It is very distinctive so that you can be sure you have the right channel. The Coast Guard broadcasts maritime safety warnings using a variety of different radio systems. This makes sure the broadcasts can be heard by all the ocean areas for which the Coast Guard is responsible.

The Coast Guard sent helicopters, aircraft, small boats, and 25 cutters to the Gulf Coast after Hurricane Katrina. They rescued 2,000 people in two days and around 33,500 people in all. The crews also assessed storm damage to offshore oil platforms and refineries.

Cutter crews must do cold-water survival training every year. Bodies lose most heat through the head, neck, groin, and sides of the chest. It's important to keep them out of cold water if you can.

Glossary

diplomacy
(dih-PLOH-muh-see)
Skill in dealing with others
without causing bad feelings.

flare (FLAYR)
A device that produces a
blaze of light used to signal,
or attract attention.

infrared (in-fruh-RED)
Light outside the visible
spectrum at its red end.

intercepting
(in-ter-SEPT-ing)
Seizing something on the way
to or before arrival.

law enforcement
(LAW in-FOR-sment)
The job of making sure that
people obey the law.

maritime
(MAR-ih-tym)
Relating to the sea.

navigation
(NA-vuh-gay-shun)
Directing the course of a ship
or aircraft.

radar (RAY-dahr)
A device that sends out radio
waves for detecting and
locating an object.

radiation (ray-dee-AY-shun)
A form of energy produced
during a nuclear reaction that
can harm humans who receive
too much of it.

real-time
(REEL-TYM)
As something is happening.

reconnaissance
(rih-KON-ih-sunz)
Spying to gain information.

rigging (RIG-ing)
Ropes, chains, and cables that
are used to control a ship's
sails and masts.

siphons (SY-funs)
Uses a bent tube to draw off
a substance from one place to
another place at a lower level.

square-rigged (SKWER-rigd)
Having sails set from poles that
sit crosswise to the masts.

synthesized (SINT-theh-syzd)
Made using a synthesizer.

vessel (VEH-sul)
A craft bigger than a rowboat
for navigation through water.

WEBSITES

Due to the changing nature of Internet links,
PowerKids Press has developed an online list of
websites related to the subject of this book.
This site is updated regularly. Please use this
link to access the list:

www.powerkidslinks.com/poc/coast/

Read More

David, Jack. *United States Coast Guard*. Torque: Armed Forces. Minneapolis, MN: Bellwether Media, 2008.

McDonnell, Julia. *Coast Guard*. US Military Forces. New York: Gareth Stevens Publishing, 2012.

Orr, Tamra B. *Your Career in the Coast Guard*. The Call of Duty: Careers in the Armed Forces. New York: Rosen Publishing, 2012.

Index